HOME AGAIN

JAMES T. FARMER III

HOME AGAIN

A RETURN TO GRACIOUS INTERIORS

Photography by EMILY FOLLOWILL

Gibbs Smith

—To the fabulous women of James Farmer Inc.
and my shop, A Place to Call Home.
—To Frank, my steady love.
—To the memory of Vic Sullivan, a great man
who loved his family beyond measure and
always made me feel that I belonged.

Contents

INTRODUCTION

The lyrics to Carole King's song "Home Again" run through my heart and mind often. The last decade has brought about a current of change for me, with many rapids I did not expect, yet the allure and comfort of home was an anchor amidst the ever-constant fluctuations.

A home changes: wallpaper and paint may fade or get an update, and a kitchen has a way of evolving from feeding a large family to scrambled eggs for two when the nest is emptier. But the essence of home is an evocative feeling of contentment and joy that no other place can supplant. The feeling of arriving home, to the place we call home, or even to celebrating home strikes a delightful chord on our heartstrings.

It may be a remodel, new shutters, or a complete overhaul, but we can still go home again. Maybe a leak leads to new wallpaper, and weather—coupled with time—wears down the back door. Perhaps the spare bedroom becomes a home office, or life catches up to us and we move from upstairs to downstairs in respect for our knees. The kids may leave but the grandchildren pile in. Family moves away and then returns. Possibly it's a new home all together for an exciting chapter's beginning. Whatever the situation, coming home again is what I am tasked with for my clients and practice for myself and family, too.

Homes evolve. They are the setting for the productions of life—ever the stage for life's happenings no matter how great or small. I often think of life in seasons. Not necessarily a demarcation of days, but more of a collection of moments set within a garden or the walls of our homes. Perhaps the season is truly a time of something blooming.

For me, the anticipation of something blooming is measured, literally, in seasons. I plant foxgloves in my garden each fall, wait for them to bolt all winter long, and then watch their eruption of tiny bell-shaped blossoms in my garden in the spring. Their growth spans three seasons, but the time they bloom in sync is the month of April. The cycle begins again when I plant caladium bulbs and sow zinnia seeds in May, knowing I'll have their lush foliage and zippy blossoms all summer long and into fall.

Seasons can be familial. A child spends the summer with a grandparent, takes swim lessons, and celebrates birthdays and holidays filled with family, wonderful meals, and times to reflect. Months and dates are not necessarily the notation of the day, but the season or collection of moments making their mark on my mind: A batch of birthdays in later spring and early summer, the holiday season at the end of the year, or the wonderful time together at our home in the mountains, a season of respite from the heat.

All these wonderful moments happen at home, in the garden, by the pool, or even under my carport, which doubles as our pavilion for summer cookouts, dinner parties, and Thanksgiving. Sometimes the dining room just runs out of room! I have a saying in my life: the same, but different. This mantra bears true for other aspects of life, as well. Recently, I had to repair a broken door. Weather and rot, the heat and cold of seasons, plus a leak culminated in replacing a door. I went with the same door—but different. The same bodes true for the kitchen update I undertook. I needed more cabinets, and an underused storage closet in the pantry became the new cabinetry.

Often, the adage of cobbler's kids not having shoes finds its way into my life as an interior designer. I needed this and that, had to repair and replace x, y, and z, so I asked my wonderful design team to assist me with their expertise. After all, we treat our clients' homes as projects with dedicated spreadsheets, CAD drawings, and lighting plans; it was time for my home to follow suit! I could not believe that a decade had passed since we moved into Farmdale. Many seasons of life were encompassed in that decade. It began with loss and ended with many gains! Give and take, ebb and flow—they all channel and course through our lives. After such a decade, it seemed appropriate to replace the door and let in a new era! And perhaps a window and some cabinets too.

Having lived at Farmdale for a decade also brought about changes in how I entertain and serve my family. Rarely these days is it a small gathering of the familiar core; my nieces and nephews are filling the seats around the table more and more. Needing a little more room and proximity to the kitchen, I rearranged my dining and living rooms. I think this is a healthy change of pace. After all, if the next decade proves the original layout superior, then I can simply go back to that! The last few years have shown me that consistency is a luxury, and adaptability is a wonderful skill set.

My garden also garnered some changes for the family's needs. With the addition of a pool, a cabana became the new epicenter of time outside. A fireplace allows us to enjoy mild winter days, and the cabana serves as en plein air headquarters for my writing assignments, lunches, summer lounging after a swim, and a simple outdoor living room. The cabana has become the narthex, of sorts, between my inner and outer sanctuaries of home and garden. It is my vestibule of creature comforts from indoors set amidst the great outdoors.

PAGE 6: For a dear client, a former home office became a lively room for a growing family. Hand-finished cypress paneling, a mahogany bowfront chest, and botanical pressings create a handsome tone.

PAGE 8: A buttery yellow ottoman and a classic Lee Jofa pattern in a fresh colorway play jauntily off a cypress-paneled family room accented with a limestone mantel designed by the home's architect, Rennie Vainstein of Cole and Cole Architects.

PRECEDING: A pair of John Rosselli tables flank the fireplace. Pottery vases turned into lamps adorn the room. Lee Jofa "Hollyhock" dresses the windows.

BELOW LEFT: The home office was originally designed by Jack Collins of Columbus, Georgia, and he had the cypress paneling finished in a honey-toned hue. We merely touched up the areas that needed it. The trellis pattern of the custom needlepoint rug is created with an oak leaf and acorn motif.

BELOW RIGHT: A custom colorway of Quadrille "Bali Hai" gives flair to club chairs and pillows.

My home in the mountains of western North Carolina, Joe Pye Cottage, also became the setting for some changes. More and more, we love to use our mountain home for celebrations and day-to-day enjoyments. Whether the rearranging of furniture or rooms, the addition of cabinetry here and there, or the actual time spent across the holidays created the realization of this home as more than a weekend retreat, it is now a true accommodation for my growing family and how we live.

As my life became more akin to those of our clients, my homes became projects for my design team to work their magic. As much as I wanted to muddle and interfere, I trusted their expertise and delighted in the changes. I often tell my clients, "You don't watch an accountant, plumber, or surgeon work their magic. So let us work ours!" But, as I learned in design school, it is rarely about creative genius, design acumen, or talent. Sure, they have their places. Yet I am constantly amazed by the mantra I was taught in school: It's 99 percent psychology, understanding your clients' lifestyle, behaviors, and needs. The rest is creativity and logistics.

That is where the head and heart intermingle in design—how to wrap our heads around sanding floors, building or moving walls, or simply how many shades of white there are when selecting cabinet colors. Home is where the heart longs to be. A house is a dwelling and a structure, while home evokes the emotions and memories of a life well lived. A home is where the seasons meld into one another, and, next thing we know, a decade has flown by and proved that life is short. But oh-so-sweet to savor the time with our family and friends in the place that welcomes us after long days, work trips, and the ever-changing rhythm of life.

The welcome of home is unlike any other salutation. Through these chapters I am delighted to take you on a tour of homes that evoke the seasons of our clients' families and set the stage for seasons to come. From the farmlands of Georgia to the Carolina Lowcountry, the Blue Ridge Mountains to the citrus groves of Florida, college towns, Martha's Vineyard, and a cottage in Mississippi, the places within these pages are inspirations and reminders of Southern style and traditional decor. Town and countryside play host and hostess, setting the tone to celebrate our homes, wherever they are.

I hope y'all are in the habit of celebrating the places you call home. It's a true privilege to work with people and families across the country, and then to create a place for my family and me in my hometown. Art and life in cadence. We can go home again—and that, my friends, is a wonderful gift to ourselves daily and through each of life's many seasons.

A Land Fairer than Day

THIS GEOGRAPHY
CARVED BY THE FALL LINE
IS AS LOVELY AND FAIR
AS OUR NECK OF THE WOODS
CAN OFFER.

The Fall Line is a geographical watershed coursing through Houston County. This watershed demarcates the direction of water flowing either to the Gulf of Mexico or the Atlantic Ocean. And with this line comes a topographic landscape, fair and lovely. Gentle hills, quintessential live oaks with Spanish moss, long-leaf pine trees, palmetto glades, and hardwood forests all intermingle where the confluence of sandy and clay soils creates an environment well suited for farming too. The opening line of the old hymn "In the Sweet By and By" melodically rings, "There's a land that is fairer than day," and I feel this geography carved by the Fall Line is as lovely and fair as our neck of the woods can offer.

Peaches and pecans along with hayfields and row crops make the south side of our county a beautiful place to call home. For some clients of mine building a new home away from town, the site for their home was one of these gentle hills amidst a setting dotted with trees. As is often the case with homes in the country, a residential structure was only the beginning. Sitings for a barn, a garden house, a pavilion, and neighboring plots for the next generations to build were all considered.

My design firm was invited to focus on the interiors, finishes, and furnishings of this homeplace. Our clients were dreaming not only of a white farmhouse with deep porches and gracious space for entertaining their large family but also craved coziness for when just the two of them were home. We were inspired by shotgun houses of the past—single-width rooms arranged one behind the other and wings unfolding off the mainline of the house—with the back garden visible through the site line of the home from the front door.

My lead designer, Jesse Noble, and associate designer Haley Yarbrough took the reigns for this project, facilitating form and function for our clients. Specific colors—blue being a favorite color of the homeowner—were interwoven in various shades and tones throughout. My team and I wanted the home to have more of a renovation feel than a new-build concept, so we incorporated elements seen in older homes. Reclaimed heart pine was used for the floors and stair banister. Sidelights and transoms at the entry vestibule created a layered front entrance. From a shotgun layout, we were able to use corridors as connectors—hyphens—from the main living and kitchen area to the bedroom and garage wings. With the central core of the home solidly arranged, the wings are reminiscent of family homes connected by dogtrots or screened porches.

With this design being rooted in a classic approach, the interior finishing and furnishings became a supporting cast for the scale, proportion, and architecture therein. The juxtaposition of complementary finishes and textures created harmony and rhythm—from stained and painted wood, brick floors, and tiled walls to light-filled rooms enveloped in deep jewel tones. We wanted our clients to yearn to be home, especially in this dwelling set lovingly and thoughtfully on a piece of land fairer than day.

PAGE 16: An X-pattern transom and sidelight entryway frames the foyer of this elegant farmhouse.

PRECEDING: For the living room, a custom EMYO painting depicts the family and a beloved dog. Reclaimed beams add texture to the ceiling. A small-scale print backs the shelves and creates a fun backdrop for books and treasures.

ABOVE: A bleached buffet anchors a vertical-plank wall in the foyer. A gold-leaf mirror adds contrast to the painted walls and the buffet's patina.

OPPOSITE: An English oak center table boasts flowers and found objects to welcome the family home; it serves as an additional dining table for the holidays. The painted paneling of the study is a soothing backdrop for antiques and upholstery.

A jute rug covers the study and is layered with a jewel-toned Oushak carpet. A Chesterfield sofa and plaid club chairs create a cozy seating area. Butterscotch gingham silk was used for the draperies and is repeated in the lampshades and accent pillows. The Lucite-and-brass light fixture adds a touch of contemporary flair and is paired with custom shades.

A Paul Montgomery mural paper envelops the dining room in soothing tones of creamy yellow, leafy green, and linen white. Lee Jofa "Hollyhock" frames the windows and is also seen on the host and hostess chairs. A notched corner ceiling detail gives definition to that plane; the design is repeated in the carpet, giving cadence to the room. One whole wall of the dining room is anchored by built-ins and a sideboard niche.

OPPOSITE: One of a pair of Italian demilunes has a faux-marble top and a delightful patina. The pottery lamps have tailored lampshades with a soft blue trim. The mural paper depicts flora and fauna fondly seen on the farm and in a nearby creek and ponds.

ABOVE: A pair of ginger jars now serve as lamps with custom shades. The built-ins create a niche for the antique mahogany sideboard set within Jacobean-inspired square paneling.

RIGHT: The view from the kitchen to the dining room is framed by a large, cased opening. A soft blue was chosen for the perimeter cabinets and shelving. Cherry butcher block tops the island.

OVERLEAF: The large island is painted a creamy white and is illuminated by two brass lanterns. Reclaimed beams add texture to the painted woodwork and contrast with the other finishes. Woven counter stools warmly pair with the heart pine floors. Open shelving breaks up the perimeter cabinetry and provides a place for displaying art and serving pieces. Cafe curtains in a cheery yellow gingham frame the view to the kitchen garden.

OPPOSITE: A graciously appointed morning bar and pantry, anchored with an antique butcher block serving as the island, lead the way to a beautiful mudroom. A bluestone floor mimics the soft blue of the kitchen cabinets and is set in an ashlar pattern.

ABOVE: The Sanderson wallpaper inspired the flax hue of the cabinets. Soapstone was used for the countertop, which is a welcome bar and buffet for entertaining. The same jaunty yellow gingham was used for cafe curtains in this space and creates visual continuity from the kitchen to the mudroom.

ABOVE AND OPPOSITE: In the laundry room, a spray of green majolica plates encircles an heirloom painting of peaches, and an Italian pottery piece hanging above brings out the citrus and foliage scene in the Schumacher "Citrus Garden" wallpaper. "Citrus Garden" is also used on the Roman shade. Shaker-style cabinetry is painted in a coordinating blue and topped with soapstone. Ample storage for additional linens and laundry items is neatly organized in this space.

ABOVE LEFT: An acanthus-leaf stripe by George Spencer is a handsome tone-on-tone pattern of olive green and creamy white. Painted chests serve as nightstands and complement the hand-carved mahogany bed created by master craftsman Andrew Reid.

ABOVE RIGHT: A gorgeous *buffet deux corps* anchors the wall opposite of the bed and is flanked by a pair of wingback chairs in a French-blue velvet. The skirted ottoman adds a flare of femininity in this handsome room. The pattern seen on the draperies and Euro pillows is "Snow Tree" by Colefax and Fowler; it sets the tone for the bathroom palette.

OPPOSITE: This primary bedroom is trimmed out in antique beams and boasts a beautiful view of the landscape beyond. A celadon, trellis-pattern wool carpet adds softness and warmth.

OPPOSITE: "Snow Tree" was used as the wallpaper and drapery in the primary bathroom, which is anchored by a stately bathtub and flanking cabinetry. The honeycomb-pattern marble floor is topped with a gorgeous gallery-style runner in shades of coral, ruby, and cerulean.

ABOVE: Louis Philippe mirrors used over both vanities provide contrast to the plumbing and cabinetry hardware. Bamboo shades in a handsome tortoiseshell finish work with the drapery panels for texture and functionality with light. A sandy white was pulled from the wallpaper for the cabinetry color and trim.

LEFT: An array of varying-width horizontal paneling envelops the grandchildren's bedroom. Contemporary art is a fine complement to the buffalo check plaid and whimsical fabric scene on the Euro pillows and draperies. Antique trunks at the foot of each twin bed have a lacquered chinoiserie finish and provide a fun place to store toys at this happy house.

ABOVE: A plaid rug in caramel and cream tones grounds the room. A twist on a traditional tapestry covers the stool and lumbar pillow. A delightful box-pleat fringe is repeated on the draperies from the Euro pillows in a warm and cheerful tomato red.

THE MIGHT OF MISSISSIPPI

"MIGHT WE MOVE TO MISSISSIPPI TOO?"
THE PARENTS PONDERED. WITH A LITTLE
MORE WEIGHING OF OPTIONS, "MIGHT"
WENT TO "MAYBE" TO "FOR SURE!" AND A
NEW ADVENTURE BEGAN.

Sometimes, a family nest seems suddenly empty of children, who all now live in a new town—not far, but across the state line, nonetheless. "Might we move to Mississippi too?" the parents pondered. With a little more weighing of options, "might" went to "maybe" to "for sure!" and a new adventure began, a move from Memphis to Oxford! The college town of Oxford, Mississippi, holds a dear place in my heart. When considering where to go to college, the lure of Ole Miss called my name; I fell head over heels for the campus and town when I visited there. But the family tradition of Auburn was too strong to resist. Years later, I was thrilled with the wonderful opportunity to work in Oxford for the loveliest family.

Our task was to recreate a homeplace for our clients—a place to welcome their children and grandchildren, invite swarms of friends on game days, and host holidays too. Their home across the state line in Tennessee had been a similar epicenter—thus, our directive. A lot in Oxford with a crumbling older home became the new homeplace, and preserving the charm of an older home while embracing the comforts of contemporary accommodations became our goal.

The original home on this site was the inspiration. The rear facade's original porch became the motivation for a sunroom and morning room off the primary bedroom. The stairwell to the new second-floor bunk room and guest room created a strong central corridor, on the main floor, and rooms with cased-opening doorways along the stairway take the line of site from the front door to the back door.

The large living room has a well of space between the kitchen and seating area, which allows for a second dining area or buffet to be set up when entertaining. Our clients love setting a buffet and bar on the island in the kitchen, which allows for the adjacent dining room and living rooms to be used for larger groups and overflow seating.

I love to create rooms for the seasons. The living room boasts a wood-burning fireplace for chilly evenings, and the sunroom is flooded with light nearly year-round. The family room can host a crowd for watching the game, and the central hallway serves as an additional dining room for larger gatherings and parties. This is a college town, and our client said it best, "We can tailgate, but in the comfort of home!"

A neutral palette of creamy white-painted paneling and woodwork, grass cloth, and heart pine flooring allow for floral draperies, velvet upholstery, and pops of artwork to truly shine. Jewel tones in carpets, fabrics, artwork, Mississippi pottery, and majolica collections inspired the colorway of the home, while reclaimed heart pine boards and beams ground and give presence above and below.

Whether our clients are hosting a large gathering or are home alone, this home is a place where they feel nested and nestled. Here their hearts truly are at peace.

PRECEDING AND ABOVE: GP & J Baker "Magnolia" is a nod to the state flower of Mississippi and the inspiration fabric for the family room. Ruby and emerald tones are juxtaposed with neutral plaids and a Stark antelope rug. French doors lead to the sunroom and balance the cased opening to the kitchen opposite. A barn by artist Kay Flierl was commissioned for the mantelpiece.

A fabulous collection of Mississippi art and pottery is on display with family heirlooms in a Welsh dresser and throughout the home. McCarty pottery, majolica, and Staffordshire all meld together beautifully. Soft white-painted paneling is perpendicular to heart pine wainscoting. The table behind the sofa and the table off the rear entry can be used for serving, dining, or as a bar when entertaining.

49

A dogtrot connecting the entries and room creates this vestibule and allows the home to function more efficiently. The trestle table can be used as a desk or set up for entertaining, and contemporary lamps add a pop of lusciousness.

OPPOSITE: The dining room is a nod to neutrality but allows art, antiques, and fabrics to work their complementary composition. Green gingham plaid by George Spencer adds a British-country touch, while Carleton V "Elise" depicts camellias on the host and hostess chairs.

ABOVE: Silver and Staffordshire classically mix on the sideboard, which is a limed oak Welsh dresser base. The mirror antique French mirror depicts a cartouche of a sheath of wheat, laurel branches, and dogwoods.

OPPOSITE: A family heirloom, the Empire sideboard anchors the corridor connecting the entryway and the stair hall. A painting by Memphis artist Emily York Ozier depicts the family at their home in Key West. Pottery vases in robin's-egg blue echo the ceiling color and carry the touch of blue in the chandelier shades, the painting, and the McCarty pottery seen here and throughout the home.

ABOVE LEFT: Etched floral hurricanes, sumptuous flowers, and paper-mache floral specimens on

pedestals create a lovely cadence in the dining room. The curves of the antique mahogany chairs are reminiscent of the curves of the Empire sideboard's backsplash.

ABOVE RIGHT: Looking through the dining room to the front parlor, a pillared, cased opening frames the view. A diamond-patterned sisal rug grounds the dining room in a neutral tone, while jewel-toned runners accent the corridors and other rooms.

PRECEDING: The kitchen island is a furniture-style legged piece. Bobbin-spooled counter stools recall the bobbin lamps with deep coral shades at the sink from Heirloom Artifacts in Nashville.

LEFT AND ABOVE: A French armchair and a Martha Washington–style armchair are two of the most comfortable chairs for a living room arranged for conversation. The blue plaid is Sister Parish. A Colefax and Fowler tone-on-tone stripe adorns the walls of the entryway and parlor. We added transoms to many of the cased openings in a nod to traditional Southern architecture. The heart pine mantel is a handsome counterpoint to floral fireside chairs and draperies. Artist Gary Bodner's Gooseneck adds a touch of whimsy to this dressier room.

ABOVE: A wooden card table anchors one end of the sunroom, making a perfect spot for bridge, mahjong, or dominoes. A trellis-patterned blue rug echoes the blue ceiling. A Cowtan and Tout indigo-hued pattern dresses the windows.

RIGHT: The sunroom has the feel of an enclosed porch. Blues, tans, and warm patinas of family antiques fill the space, along with our clients' fantastic collection of majolica plates displayed on the wall. Ceiling fans are a further nod to the porch inspiration, and lamps provide softer light for evening reading and cards.

OPPOSITE: In the primary bedroom, soothing tones of brown and aqua create a balance of handsome and feminine styles. The Schumacher draperies echo the color scheme in an oak leaf and acorn motif. The custom mahogany bed was hand carved.

LEFT AND BELOW: This area allows for slow mornings to preside or a place of respite in the evening. The feel here is to be like an enclosed porch. Cabinetry and built-ins hide the television. A family heirloom corner cabinet anchors one end of the morning room off the primary bedroom.

ABOVE: In the bunk room upstairs, cubbies with book nooks were created for the grandchildren. A palette of tomato red and cadet blue is inspired by the Ole Miss colors—a nod to the family's alma mater and the town.

RIGHT: Drawers under the bunks provide storage for toys and clothes. The navy animal-print rug is a soft, woven loop pile, perfect for watching a movie. Brass lights in each bunk make reading after dark a fun activity. A Sister Parish star pattern is papered on the sloped ceilings of each bunk and is used as fabric for the Euro-style pillows.

THE
LOVELIEST
VILLAGE

CREATING A FEELING OF HOME
WITHIN A CONDO TOWER—
MEANT WE HAD SOME . . .
AMAZING OPPORTUNITIES.

Being a third-generation Auburn alum, I call any excuse to work in my college hometown a treat! When dear clients decided to create a place to call home there, I was nearly giddy! The couple had gone to Auburn as well, so our connection to the college was a driving force for this location. The new place was not a traditional homesite, however. An entire floor of a new condo tower set right downtown and by the campus was to be the new home. Creating a feeling of home amidst a bustling area—and within a condo tower—meant we had some design challenges, yet amazing opportunities in turn. The views of the downtown sights and the college campus are awesome! We wanted to embrace and frame those views while creating a sense of home within.

Truly, we started with steel beams and a slab! Our first task was to create a floor plan, casings, and structural elements that bent more toward the traditional. A niche in the main hallway created a proper foyer, and demarcating spaces with passages and loads of custom cabinetry made this big, open space start to feel more traditional in its layout and function. Adding wall coverings and custom lighting along with bringing in antiques with terrific patina began to round off the finishes and set the tone for the furnishings. The warmth that antique pieces bring to a mix of vintage and new furniture is the hallmark of mixing textures and tones that we love to embrace.

From the bedrooms appointed for guests and family, to the living room and kitchen flowing into one another for entertaining and watching sporting events, this house became a home within a matter of days after we installed the furnishings. A home with a traditional layout was created within a more contemporary shell, and the best of both worlds came together in comfort and design. Blues, aquas, greens, and punches of yellow became the palette for the home, allowing artwork, collections of majolica, and upholstery to take their places in this framework. One of my favorite areas we designed was the butler's pantry behind the kitchen, which allowed the kitchen to be more open for entertaining and storage. Smaller appliances and a wine fridge are tucked into this fun new space.

Another area that took our attention was the ceilings. In a typical condo, the dedicated electrical, plumbing, HVAC ductwork, chases, and piping that serve the whole building are givens. This made some definite decisions on wall placement. However, the ceilings in this condo could be dropped a tad, and this slight lowering allowed us to add treatments with rafters, wallpaper, and great color, as well as handsome crown molding. The ceilings have some lovely moments not often seen in a contemporary setting like this.

Being in downtown Auburn and close to great restaurants and collegiate attractions allows our clients to walk to dinner, tailgate, and embrace all this proximity offers. It has given the family a fun new reality. There is even a grocery store downtown within easy walking distance. So, the family truly has a place in town with an urban feel, not far from the countryside.

With this project being smack in the heart of downtown, I could not help but think how I used to pass this place every single day on my walk to campus. Collegiate James, learning the design trade, would one day be a designer and bring those college memories to the present.

PAGES 66–67: A coffee table still life features a majolica plate depicting an oak leaf and acorns—a nod to the Toomer's oaks planted across the street from this home.

PRECEDING: An aqua-hued raffia grass cloth envelops the living area of this home. We created demarcation in this condominium with beams and cased openings, cabinetry, and wallcoverings to make the spaces feel more grounded and architectural. A color palette of marigold yellow, greens, creams, and tan is accented with blue plaid and a floral depicting the same hues. A plaid rug grounds the space.

OPPOSITE: A large antique draper's table from France anchors a long wall. The television is treated like a framed piece of art along a gallery wall of pressed botanicals, brackets, and jars. A French watercolor over the TV is reminiscent of Auburn's art museum's collection of early 20th-century art.

Framed botanicals by artist Lauren Lachance create a grid over the tufted sofa in a deep saffron velvet. The Ming-style coffee table is wrapped in an indigo grass cloth and lacquered. Leather chairs, ottomans, and a faux bois–patterned chair provide further seating. A pair of lattice-framed mirrors were repainted to match the trim and tone of the nearby kitchen cabinets.

OPPOSITE: The slab-style drawer fronts and cabinetry harken to British styles seen in country estates. The brass bin pulls echo the warmth of tones in the adjacent living room. A gallery runner in tomato red, aqua, and celadon runs the length of the range wall. The marble slab used for the perimeter countertops is run perpendicular as a backsplash, showing the veining on the two surfaces.

ABOVE: The coffee bar and pantry anchor the center wall of the kitchen. The large island has a pub table at one end for in-house dining. With so many restaurants merely steps away in this collegiate downtown, we allocated space for a butler's pantry and more storage beyond.

OVERLEAF LEFT: The long wall opposite the range wall is grounded by a whitewashed antique French enfilade. Woven rattan lamps, a collection of copper molds, majolica, an antique oil painting, and a barometer create a sensational display. A Chelsea Textiles print is gathered and pleated for the lampshades.

OVERLEAF RIGHT: A butler's pantry is awash in deep hues of teal, aqua, and turquoise. Ample storage for entertaining pieces is concealed in the cabinetry. A William Morris willow leaf–motif paper dresses the walls, while striped paper adorns the ceiling, complete with a sunburst light fixture.

ABOVE: An entry vestibule off the elevator hallway is now a proper foyer, where an English lowboy is offset with a Louis Philippe mirror and pottery lamps. The trellis-patterned grass cloth gives the space texture and dimension. Painted wooden tiles are set on the diagonal, a classic design distinguishing the space.

OPPOSITE: Jesse Noble, my lead designer, had the idea to create a niche from what would have been a superfluous hall closet. Here, we were able to create a vignette in the long hallway. A French buffet, vases turned into lamps, and a painting by Bee Sieburg create a welcoming scene. The octagonal mirror reflects the collection of botanicals and Coleen Rider sconces.

OPPOSITE: A hashed-pattern wallcovering by Elizabeth Dow creates visual texture in this guest suite. The blue and tan color scheme is continued with the drapery and floor covering.

ABOVE LEFT: Cowtan and Tout linen draperies depict dahlias, one of the homeowners' favorite flowers. The striped rug is from Elizabeth Eakins.

ABOVE RIGHT: The guest suite bathroom is awash in shades of French blue and robin's-egg blue. Custom cabinetry seen here and throughout the home is designed by Melanie Herrington, my associate designer and talented teammate. The fretwork cabinet doors and paneled drawers make a distinctive foundation for the marble top and backsplash.

ABOVE: A Ming-style foot and return elevate this custom cabinetry. A handsome scalloped mirror, Lucite and brass sconces, and colorful artwork create a cheerful vignette.

OPPOSITE: Creamy yellow with warm, inky sepia is such a handsome combination. Upholstered twin beds in yellow and white are offset with a hand-painted brown and white chest. Antique brass candlesticks are wired as lamps, with a delightful sunburst pattern for shades. The tone-on-tone striped paper adds visual texture, while the mirror with birds and bunnies and pear tree branches adds a touch of whimsy and reflects artwork by Lindsey J Porter.

OPPOSITE: In the primary suite, a scalloped headboard is upholstered in Sister Parish "Dolly" in a fresh new colorway. Nickel nailheads create a banded pattern around the perimeter of the bed and headboard. A large-scale fern-motif grass cloth creates a dramatic background for a series of antique bird prints as well as tan checks and lighter blues seen throughout the room.

ABOVE: A favorite trick of the trade, we used the same Sister Parish "Dolly" pattern on the bed, chairs, drapery, and lampshades.

ABOVE: Anchoring one end of the bedroom is a dresser hand-painted in marshmallow white with chocolate-brown banding. A carved mirror of gold and brown adds a handsome element to this space. Ceramic vases are converted into lamps, with "Dolly" as their pleated fabric shades. A club chair is both practical and cozy for taking in the window views.

OPPOSITE: "Dolly" is used as wallcovering in the primary bathroom. A crisp white marble tiles the floor and the shower. A deep tub is flanked by antique sconces and artichoke plates in this soothing setting. A nearly abstract French landscape and harbor scene hangs over the tub.

A FAMILY AFFAIR

CLASSIC PATTERNS WITH UPDATED
COLORWAYS, MORE CONTEMPORARY
ART MIXED WITH VINTAGE FINDS,
AND FURNITURE PLACED FOR
EVERYDAY LIVING—AS WELL AS
ENTERTAINING—WERE ARRANGED
FOR THIS FAMILY.

Dear friends of mine called about a new project in Birmingham. They had a growing family and found a home that would suit their burgeoning nest. The previous owners had completed an extensive remodel, and the new home was an updated canvas ready for finishes, papers, and furnishings. Birmingham is one of my absolute favorite towns, as I have many friends from Auburn there and a branch of my grandfather's family, too. It has always felt like home to me, and the chance to create a home there was a delightful opportunity.

Having known the wife's family (her sister-in-law and I are from the same hometown) our friendship and familial ties set the foundation for this design project. Traditional tones, lovely antique pieces, fresh approaches to old-school design, and fun doses of color became inspirational aspects. Classic patterns with updated colorways, more contemporary art mixed with vintage finds, and furniture placements for everyday living—as well as entertaining—were arranged for this family.

From the ample foyer and stair hall to the formal and informal dining rooms, this home has a flow from one room to the next that is as suitable for cocktail parties with friends or hosting holidays as it is for a Saturday morning pancake breakfast. Rooms designed for seasons work perfectly here. The fireplace is probably the main attraction during the colder months, and the French doors open in springtime to bring the outdoors inside during those lovely months. The rear terrace flows across the back of the home and becomes a perfect place to spill over for larger crowds.

A springboard for this design scheme came from the dining room's amazing scenic paper. I was able to pull those threads across the home and envelop the other rooms with coordinating colors. The dining room furnishings feature a suite of salmon-toned draperies, upholstery, and cushions. For the adjoining living room, the lighter tones and softer jewel tones from the dining room paper take hold on the upholstery and wallcovering. As with salt bringing out the sweetness, a contrast in colors adds a visual sensation and complement. The slightly more feminine colors in the dining room allow for more saturated, masculine versions of these colors to fall into place in the family room, seen through the dining and living rooms. Clever folding doors in a handsome stain and polish separate the rooms and reflect the patina of the antique tables and chairs.

As the family room boasts similar shades inspired by the dining room but with deeper tones, corals become a deeper persimmon and red is used in the artwork and antique screen hung on the wall. Tomato, silver-blue, and creamy white paneling and ceiling woodwork blend with the glazed brick floors and grass cloth on the walls.

The kitchen and family dining room take on a lighter and brighter air, with the dining space enveloped in a trellis-patterned grass cloth. I wanted the family's everyday dining space to have the feel of a porch with brick floors and a sunny window that had been closed in over the years. This room is also the vestibule connecting the front foyer to the kitchen and becomes a great space for entertaining, with its own buffet and bar. The kitchen and dining room are connected by swinging doors with antique brass plates for a functional and nostalgic way to open rooms to one another.

The zippy green paper and Chippendale banister in the foyer are complemented with deep jewel-toned rugs—a foretaste of the dining room's colors. A trellis stair runner leading to the family bedrooms was inspired by the fanlight transom over the front door.

A more handsome respite in warm tones of brown, sepia, and camel provides the scheme for a home office and den. Slate blue floral and plaid complement the brown sugar–hued grass cloth walls. Pottery and carved stone lamps alongside framed antique prints and a waterfall glass coffee table fulfill their roles as tasked accessories and juxtapositions.

This is a happy home for a lovely family with three little girls. I wanted to create a space that would be timeless. I can see the daughters posing for school dances along the stairwell and family dinners around the tables in both dining spaces, and I can hear the stories and laughter that fill these rooms from season to season. The vision for this house was to create a comfortable home for my friends, and my design team executed that vision marvelously.

PRECEDING AND OPPOSITE: In the foyer, antiques such as pressed botanicals, a French commode, and a Louis Phillipe mirror add warm layers to the tone-on-tone paper. An English faux-bamboo bench is a good perch in this gallery. The newel posts and handrails are painted silvery green, a shade similar to the grass cloth in the adjoining living room.

ABOVE: The fireside seating reflects coordinating fabrics, with an antique Chinese coffee table anchoring the space. An abstract by Colleen Leach was commissioned for over the mantel.

OPPOSITE: A classic GP & J Baker pattern, "Oriental Bird," is set on velvet for the sofa and completed with a bullion fringe.

OVERLEAF: Buttery, almost citrine-colored leather chairs pull from the shades in the dining room paper, while tones of coral, salmon, and peach are reflected in the artwork, hurricane lamps on the mantel, and glazed ceiling. Antique ceramic jars make for wonderful lamp bases. I believe no good lamp starts life as a lamp!

THIS SPREAD: The Zoë Design hand-painted wallpaper was the springboard for the entire home's color palette. From salmon silk draperies and lampshades to the salmon "Bali Hai" pattern on the host and hostess chairs and the salmon plaid on the side chairs, I brought out the citrus, peach, and persimmon seen in the paper's scenic sprawl.

A black chinoiserie sideboard anchors one wall with a stately mirror above, which reflects the French doors and chandelier. A muted blue-gray ceiling allows the paper and fabrics to have their moment with color and saturation.

My dear friend Mary Cox Brown worked her magic with the florals seen throughout.

PRECEDING AND OPPOSITE: The family room has two sofas back-to-back, dividing the room into two seating areas. One area is a cozy spot for television and fires, while the other is more for conversation and reading.

ABOVE LEFT: A graciously scaled, carved-frame mirror reflects the room beautifully and is anchored below with a long enfilade, providing the perfect display area for family photos and seasonal blossoms.

ABOVE RIGHT: The drapery panels are enlivened with vines and floral motifs in colors seen through the room. A sisal rug unifies the entire space, while a tribal runner is layered in each seating area. Imari vases were made into lamps. Brass reading lamps provide further lighting, while a gold-and-bronze fixture illuminates the room. The artwork above the mantel was found at Toby West Home in Cashiers.

ABOVE: In the everyday dining space, shelves display jaunty pieces of majolica and oyster plates and are underpinned with a custom banquette in a happy, French blue plaid. The antique Murano chandelier depicts pretty daffodils. The lemon and orange artwork is by Gretchen Kelly, and the abstract is by Nancy B. Westfall.

OPPOSITE: This room is also the vestibule connecting the front foyer to the kitchen, and it becomes a great space for entertaining, with its own buffet and bar. The French buffet boasts two woven-ceramic jars made into lamps, with shades of the same fabric as on the banquette.

OPPOSITE: The banquette, constructed by Grant Trick, runs the length of the family dining room. An antique French table adds a warm patina. Contemporary artwork adds a pop of color, while rattan chairs harken to the feel of an enclosed porch.

ABOVE: The kitchen is awash in various shades of white, from the trim to the countertops to the tiled backsplash. The window shade fabric is by J. P. Horton Textiles. Carlton V "Indienne Quince" graces the kitchen walls.

OPPOSITE: In the office-den, slate blue floral and plaid fabrics complement the brown sugar–hued grass cloth walls. Sepia-toned landscape prints and a tobacco-hued mohair camelback sofa anchor the room.

ABOVE: On the opposite wall, an English "two over three" block chest is juxtaposed with a gold leaf mirror with a reed-and-ribbon motif.

HIGH STYLE
IN THE
LOWCOUNTRY

ON A POINT SURROUNDED BY
MARSHES AND MARITIME FORESTS OF
SPANISH MOSS–LADEN LIVE OAKS AND PALMETTO,
OUR CLIENTS FOUND THEIR NEW HOME
FOR RETIREMENT AND A NEW SEASON.

For a couple finding "home again" and a wonderful new chapter in life, my design team was blessed with a delightful opportunity. Along the marshes and inland waterways of the South Carolina Lowcountry, vistas of spartina grass and sunsets are framed with Spanish moss–laden live oaks and palmetto forests. Here, on a point surrounded by these maritime forests and marshes, our client found their new home for retirement, family gatherings, and a new season.

The decision to relocate from town to country was not made lightly. When this property became available, our clients knew this was the place for them. The challenge was how to finish and furnish a new home to feel as if the family had always lived there and how to further enhance the surroundings. The Lowcountry is nearly incomparable with vistas and colors and skies, so, naturally, the marsh became our inspiration.

Greens and sepia tones, accents of blue, earthen hues, and textures from seagrass rugs, grass cloth wallcoverings, and the rich patina of antiques all melded into formation with a mural of the marsh painted by artist Karen Larson Turner. Tonal shades of white-painted paneling allow the reclaimed heart pine floors to ground the rooms in a honey-toned hue. Accents of tobacco brown, delft blue, and marshy green are carried throughout the home and artwork.

With the formal dining and living open to the family area and more relaxed side of the home, we were careful to create threads of continuity with the color schemes and textures. A fabric of caramel and cream oak leaves dresses all the windows and French doors of these open-concept spaces. Shades of darker browns and greens with blue accents are then repeated in each space for complementary compositions and common ground. Antique brass tables, burnished-gold mirrors and sconces, and framing blend with heart pine beams and newel posts.

The living room area features a baby grand piano—the perfect place for holiday parties and dinner serenades. This family graciously entertains, and the living room is the perfect launch pad for celebrations to commence. A scenic pattern of marsh birds, lotus flowers, and grasses adds to the family room palette and character too. The backs of the shelving are papered in a favorite pheasant pattern that provides the collections with a wonderful backdrop. Diamond-pattern sisal rugs ground the spaces and define the furniture groupings.

PAGES 110—111: Elevated plant stands hold parlor palms as a nod to surrounding palmettos just beyond the grounds of this home.

PRECEDING: A George III mahogany sideboard with yew wood inlay is the handsome foundation for the fabulous mural. It boasts blue-and-white jars as lamps and a collection of silver pieces in elegant Southern style.

RIGHT: The mantel boasts a sunset scene from the property by Millie Gosch. A landscape by the late artist Marianne Dunn is displayed on a console—one of a pair of demilune tables with a garland and medallion frieze on the apron. A silky velvet animal print from Jane Shelton dresses a French chair. Grass-inspired light fixtures visually anchor the volume above the dining, living, and family rooms.

The billiard room and its adjoining bar are awash in sunlight from the copious windows and French doors. Painted V-groove paneling is contrasted with stained heart pine trim and paneling wainscoting. This lighter and brighter palette above the chair rail allows the artwork collections, mirrors, and window draperies to shine. A seating area of four club chairs and an ottoman is the perfect vestibule between the gardens outside and the billiard table and bar.

In the study, just off the billiard room, cypress envelops the space with wall paneling, built-ins, and beams. Two commissioned pieces by Dirk Walker flank the cased opening to the billiard room and are reminiscent of quail hunts in the Lowcountry. An antique Italian painted-leather screen is backdrop for the Chesterfield velvet sofa and sets the color palette for the room into motion.

A collection of guest suites are located on either end of the home, each a delightful composition of greens and blues and inspired by the marsh and landscape just beyond the windows. The suites are arranged for grandchildren, siblings, parents, and visiting friends, accordingly. Two rooms are swathed in gorgeous shades of green—painted paneling and grass cloth—with stunning views to the marsh and gardens. Two other guest rooms are enveloped in raffia wallcovering with blue undertones and fabrics.

The primary suite is a nod to the homeowners' favorite shades of blue and green and their prized antiques. From indigo hues to sage green, this room is a respite and perfect place to start and end each day—especially with expansive views onto the marsh. A woven sisal wall treatment in a shade of taupe that blends so well with spartina grass is the backdrop for the four-poster bed.

The home and property are cherished and lovingly maintained for family functions, outdoor sports, and entertaining. For my design team and me, the task was a labor of love, intertwining the best of the Lowcountry with luxurious, Southern-style interior design. Our clients are a dream team, trusting us to facilitate their new place—finding home again amidst the marsh's beauty.

OPPOSITE: Tones of sweet grass make up the color palette in varying shades of tawny neutral and soothing green. The Paolo Moschino oak leaf and acorn fabric creates a wonderful trellis pattern for the drapery and upholstered pieces. Custom mirrors depict deer grazing on hostas, which could be a familiar sight just outside the doors too.

ABOVE: A pantry behind supports the galley kitchen with storage, prep space, and extra refrigeration. My design team added sliding glass cabinet doors, which are suitable in a tight gallery space and allow for china and dishes to be on display and easily accessed.

OPPOSITE: A pair of copper-and-bronze custom lanterns sport plumes of marsh grass. The tone-on-tone counter stool fabric by Carleton V depicts deer, rabbits, and turtles.

OVERLEAF LEFT: The formal and informal dining spaces run perpendicular to one another and display English formality and informality accordingly for each.

OVERLEAF RIGHT: The family room built-ins are backed in at Twigs "Pheasant" paper, a handsome backdrop for antique books, tea caddies, and shells. A pair of English landscape oil paintings crest the top shelves and carry color and texture upward. A marsh scene painted by Millie Gosch was inspired by the dock just beyond this room. Schumacher "Lotus Garden" comes alive on the club chairs and pillows.

PRECEDING AND ABOVE: Open to the billiard room is a full-bayed sitting room with ample sunlight. I love to use four club chairs and a round ottoman in a space like this.

OPPOSITE: For the billiard room and bar, my team and I created a fun destination for our clients and their guests. We painted the bar and cabinetry to match the painted paneling and contrast with heart pine floors and wainscoting and the bar-back countertops. A collection of antique English, French, and Italian oil paintings creates a stately gallery wall. A faux-bamboo billiard light by Paul Ferrante gives a British West Indies vibe, while a vintage tole sculpture of cattails was transformed into a statement lamp.

LEFT: In the study, a painted, antique Italian leather screen serves as backdrop for the Chesterfield velvet sofa. Muddy greens, deep teals, sky blues, and warm wooden tones are juxtaposed with deep terra-cotta, brighter blue, and deeper azure in the antique Persian rug.

ABOVE: The mantel is carved from pecky cypress. Deep teal grass cloth backs the shelves displaying artwork, beloved books, and sentimental accessories.

ABOVE: We treated each bedroom suite in colors suited for their direction and view. Here, an aqua-and-cream raffia wallcovering is offset with creamy white paneling and handsome mahogany, walnut, and painted furnishings. Accents of robin's egg in the artwork, drapery, and bedding make for a cheery setting.

OPPOSITE: The primary suite opens to a lovely screened porch with incomparable marsh views. The mahogany "Rice Bed" is carved with rice stalks on the posts in an homage to a Lowcountry tradition. A tightly woven sisal grass cloth covering the walls recalls the tones of the spartina grass in the marsh. A pair of caned-and faux-bamboo chairs provide seating. The drapery fabric mimics palm fronds and lotus flowers in a concentric pattern.

PRECEDING: A contemporary take on a classic four-poster bed is painted and glazed in a linen white, which is repeated on the trim in this guest suite. The luscious green on the paneling was replicated in the custom colorway of the bench and draperies, which have a vibrant blue trim accent on the leading edges.

ABOVE LEFT: A custom-painted dresser in milk chocolate brown and white is delightfully offset against the soothing green walls. An antique pier mirror depicts waterfowl in its gilded frame.

ABOVE RIGHT: One of the favorite secretaries I have ever found, this English mahogany piece is a substantial anchor in this suite. A collection of books, prints, and heirlooms are displayed, and a trio of demijohns crests the top.

OPPOSITE: The gallery-style Jack and Jill bathroom off two of the guest suites is awash in a mineral blue paper depicting water fowl and lotuses. An English oak "trolley" is used as a towel rack and accent piece. I love the patina of antique oak, mahogany, walnut, and cherry against blues and greens.

ABOVE: For this guest suite, a woven raffia wallcovering of silvery greens and sepia wraps the room above the painted wainscoting. I found the fabulous faux-bamboo chest from my friend Ellie Proctor. Artwork by Madison Brooks flanks the piece, while a shell-encrusted mirror reflects the room. Ocmulgee Arts executed the framing seen throughout.

RIGHT: The blue-and-white Scalamandré linen drapery depicts pines and waterfowl reminiscent of the Lowcountry. A pair of Italian demilunes serve as bedside tables, and the custom faux-bamboo bed is painted and glazed in a silvery white. The family's custom logo of a heron in marsh grass is embroidered on the bed linens and is seen throughout the home.

A Not
Too Far-Off
Place

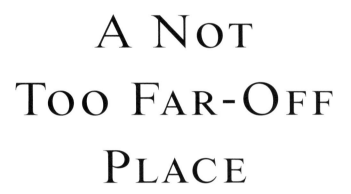

A MOVE JUST DOWN THE STREET.
A NOT-TOO-FAR-OFF PLACE TO CALL HOME
WAS THE ENDEAVOR FOR THIS FAMILY.
YOU CAN GO HOME AGAIN—
EVEN IN THE SAME NEIGHBORHOOD.

Some friends and clients in the enclave of Orlando, Florida, known as Winter Park were quite content on a tree-lined street close to family and friends. That is, until "the house we would buy if it ever came up for sale" happened to come on the market. Not a far-off move—a matter of a few houses down the street—this home provided a lakefront view and additional room. I ran into these clients at a favorite antique shop in Cashiers, North Carolina, where we both have second homes, and the possibility of this home coming up for sale was discussed. Next thing we know, the new house is an official project.

Painting the exterior brick and adding a tile roof gave the home charm and character in this established neighborhood. From a formal dining room and living room to a sunroom across the back, the updated floor plan has made the home a delight for entertaining.

The foyer and front hall are not only the entrance into the home but serve as a gallery of art and display. The Chippendale wainscoting adds pattern and character. A printed grass cloth adorns the walls. Deep ruby and watermelon reds are found in the entry runner, which foreshadows the tones in the adjoining front parlor. Here, Chinese red coffee tables mimic the rug in the entry and flank seating areas anchored with sofas in peach damask. The statement artwork of a spoonbill bird (page 140) by John Costin was the launch pad for this room's palette. The ceiling is a sensational robin's-egg blue with bamboo molding, thus creating a fantastic fretwork pattern.

A new kitchen became the epicenter of the home, and from here, I was able to weave a color story of soft citrus hues, deep greens, and punches of coral throughout the home. A breakfast room opens onto the new lattice-clad sunroom and circles back around the living room. Greens and oranges in many shades playfully unite from room to room.

The green lattice in the sunroom enhances the perception; we wanted it to look and feel like a glazed-in porch. Wicker and rattan furniture in peaches and greens rest comfortably on an abaca woven rug atop the reclaimed brick floors. Pieces of Florida Highwaymen art can be seen throughout the home.

A stunning, custom Gracie hand-painted chinoiserie wallpaper is the highlight in the dining room. Custom hand-painted consoles complement the antique patina of the table and sideboard under the window.

The kitchen palette extends into the adjoining family room with a deeper tone. Deep green velvet sofas and a velvet divan provide ample seating, while two velvet club chairs depict a marshland scene of waterfowl and flora. A pickled pecky cypress ceiling is a nod to Old Florida loggias and porches.

Pecky cypress covers the ceiling of the primary suite as well, which is awash in aqua and green. A faux-bamboo bed is finished in a sandy white hue. A foliage pattern creates rhythm and cadence in the draperies and continues the soothing scheme of soft aqua, blues, and greens. In the dressing area and primary bath, the palette continues from the primary bedroom.

In a very special bedroom, we were tasked with creating a sanctuary for our clients' daughter. Since their baby girl would grow so much from when we started the renovation until the day the family moved into this home, we selected a "big girl" bed that she would grow into and have forever. A salmon-pink trellis wallpaper creates fun pattern in the room.

A move down the street. A not-too-far-off place to call home. That was the endeavor for this family. You can go home again—even in the same neighborhood!

PAGES 136–137: Cased openings frame the view from the front parlor to the foyer and dining room beyond. Applied faux-bamboo molding in a Greek key return adorns the ceiling. A pair of *sang de boeuf* coffee tables add a handsome touch to the pops of peach, coral, and blue.

PRECEDING: A Sister Parish palm frond–motif grass cloth gives a nod to the flora just outside. An Italian commode with a deep-emerald marble anchors the foyer wall.

ABOVE AND OPPOSITE: A spoonbill painting by John Costin directed the colorful accents of the room. Peach damask sofas were custom built by Grant Trick with dressmaker detail. Abstract art by Beth Berss.

PRECEDING: The custom Gracie wallpaper is reminiscent of an Old Florida club and fond memories there. An antique Venetian glass chandelier lights the dining room with delight. Chinese Chippendale chairs, a collection of rose medallion china in the cabinets, and hand-carved hurricanes round out the room elegantly. Citrine silk draperies frame the window, echoing the vivid citrine in the wallpaper.

The corner cabinets and wainscoting were original to the home, and a new coat of jade green brought out their details. We reworked the hardware.

OPPOSITE: The dining room ceiling is lacquered in a beautiful peach tone, while hand-painted consoles echo that color as well.

ABOVE LEFT: A Queen Anne–style mirror handsomely contrasts with the wallpaper. The painted consoles are by John Rosselli. Shirred silk shades and cord elegantly coordinate with the lamps.

ABOVE RIGHT: An antique foot bath serves as the perfect vessel for palm fronds, hydrangeas, and roses.

PRECEDING AND THESE PAGES: We opened the kitchen and family room to one another with a large cased opening flanked by pantry and storage cabinetry designed by my team. The large island is paneled in pecky cypress—a nod to the history and provenance of Old Florida homes and clubs. Reclaimed brick was used for the kitchen, breakfast, and sunroom floors for the feel of an enclosed porch or summer kitchen. Schumacher banana leaf wallpaper adds a lively tone of citrine and citrus hues. The lighting is by Urban Electric.

A custom needlepoint area rug and stair runner anchor the living room and stairwell. We used pickled pecky cypress on the ceiling. Emerald, mossy, and teal greens were used for the furniture with accents of tiger, lotus flowers, and trellis motifs in pillows. The divan is a lounge spot favored by our clients' daughter.

In the breakfast room, we wanted to create a bay window moment to extend the view and footprint toward the lake. Nearly 180-degree views of the landscape and water can be seen now from the kitchen and breakfast room. A custom colorway of Quadrille "Lyford Trellis" dresses the windows. I love how the bay window, table, and rug create a cadence of concentric patterns and shapes.

ABOVE: The latticework of the sunroom frames the breakfast area in this delightful vignette.

OPPOSITE: A favorite piece of Florida Highwaymen art is seen over a decoupaged chest from Vivianne Metzger Antiques. A vintage melon jar was turned into a lamp base. I used a cord on the sugary silk shade for added pop.

OVERLEAF: My team drew the plans to enclose a former screened porch and then designed the trellis and latticework.

All painted out in a soothing green, the latticework creates architecture and pattern in this room. A bleached French buffet is juxtaposed with a gold-leaf mirror. Vintage ceramic cockatoos were made into lamps with custom lampshades. Wicker and rattan furnishings give a nod to the porch. Elephant garden stools add flair and personality. The Lee Jofa floral pillows have a seashell trim, a whimsical touch for the Sunshine State.

OPPOSITE: Contemporary lamps and nightstands flank the faux- bamboo bed. Florida Highwaymen art is also seen in the primary suite. A printed grass cloth, banana leaf needlepoint cushions, and a loquat leaf–motif drapery all work together for a place of soothing respite. The lightly pickled pecky cypress ceiling adds a nostalgic touch to older South Florida homes.

ABOVE: A hibiscus still life by a Florida Highwayman artist adds a pop of color to this reading niche in the primary suite. A green-and-white cabana stripe upholsters the chair and is accented with a needlepoint banana leaf lumbar. French doors lead to the terrace and pool.

ABOVE: An updated chintz by Cowtan and Tout depicting fish, lotus flowers, and other flora is used on the draperies and vanity stool. Antique brass sconces, drapery hardware, and plumbing fixtures add warmth.

OPPOSITE: In the primary suite's bathroom, I duplicated "Talavera" by Brunschwig & Fils from the bedroom window drapery as the wallcovering and bench and ottoman upholstery too. This wonderful pattern creates a damask-like effect of loquat leaves. White marble tile is set on the diagonal. The gallery connecting the bedroom and bathroom is a lovely connector, or "hyphen," between rooms.

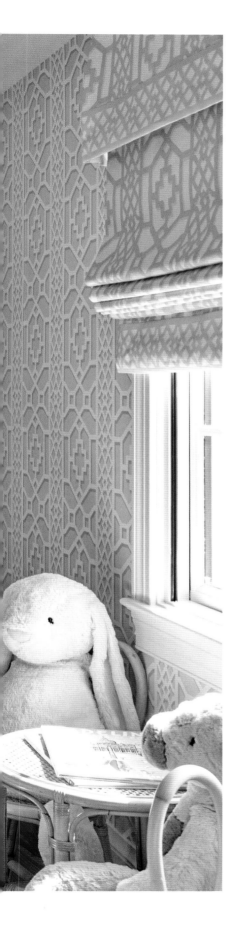

We wanted to create a "big girl" room for our clients' daughter. She was just a toddler when we started the renovation, and we wanted a room for her to grow up with. The salmon-hued "Zanzibar Trellis" by Schumacher creates the perfect backdrop on the walls and windows. A peacock wicker chair, grass cloth–wrapped nightstands, and a diamond trellis rug round out the furnishings. The headboard upholstery is a seashell motif by famed interior designer Dorothy Draper.

HOME AGAIN, AGAIN

IF I HAVE LEARNED ONE THING
ABOUT LIFE, IT IS THAT
THE CURRENT CAN SHAPE YOU—
BUT YOU DON'T HAVE TO LET IT
DROWN YOU! SO, AFTER A DECADE OF
LIVING AT FARMDALE,
IT WAS TIME FOR A CHANGE.

I want to be home again and feeling right, . . ." Carole King wrote and sang. My mother listened to Carole King so much that her tunes are not only the soundtrack to my childhood, but a one-way ticket to happy memories of home.

A lot of life happened in a decade for me. I lost my grandmother and mother in the same year—right at the onset of building Farmdale. My home became not just my house, but a place my sisters could come home to, bring their families, celebrate holidays, and even have a wedding. I donated a kidney to my sister Meredith and, three years later, she and Keaton were married in the garden. Sister Maggie and her husband Zach had two children—and adopted three more! Our family grew—from the three siblings left in the wake of our mother's death—to a bustling bunch of kinsmen redeemers!

My aunt and uncle, who also live on our property, became our parents and grandparents to the children, with my first cousins becoming more like siblings. If I have learned one thing about life, it is that the current can shape you—but do not let it drown you. So, after a decade of living at Farmdale, it was time for a change. The current was no longer a riptide or rapids, but a steady stream of nieces and nephews, lovely holidays, garden blossoms, pool parties, and happiness. And even meeting someone special myself. A full nest to an empty nest to just the two of us—steady and good. The changes at hand were welcomed and exciting—and, of course, as with some of the best home projects, started not with a plan, but with a leak!

When water started trickling down a wall, I used this as an excuse to redo the wallpaper. Where water had been seeping through a wall and door, it was time for a new door . . . doors . . . and maybe a new kitchen? I did not set out to redo my kitchen, but the timing presented itself. So I anchored my choices in the classics—traditional and proven elements—the same, but different. Creamy linen-white cabinets replaced the open shelves, walnut changed out the pine countertops, and we created a bit more room in the pantry for the odds and ends that kitchens seem to accrue.

I believe kitchens should be pretty but useful—not sterile laboratories. As with all my projects, I use stone and wood for countertops, and here, my collection of creamware, tureens,

and *soupières* is on display—along with favorite cookbooks—flanking the front window. A mossy, sage green gives the island some color and character—and I love how this color shifts with the seasons. My work triangle did not change, per se, but I was able to keep the footprint nearly the same—but different—in how we use the space. I serve off the stove and island, and this flow works for us. The island serves as our supper spot when it's only the two of us, but when the herd descends upon Farmdale, I set up a long table in the carport.

My island is the buffet these days, and I needed a bit more room around the table. My dining room became my living room, and the new dining room is right off the kitchen where I can squeeze the family around the table with a high chair or booster seat, or two! I found that some of us linger around the table, and some of us roost in the living room. I love having the big windows looking out to the front yard, and the living room has become my "morning room." It's cozy for two or twelve, and the color scheme of green, peach, and floral draperies reminds me of my mother's living room from my childhood.

In the midst of the remodel of my kitchen, my contractor called and said, "You can go home again," after some sanding and painting had kicked me out for a few days. And so I have gone home again. It's the same place and filled with memories—and set for a new chapter with many happy seasons to come.

PRECEDING: The two seating groups allow for my family and friends to gather and converse. Each grouping is anchored by paneled screens in the most gorgeous terra-cotta, cream, and apricot hues.

ABOVE: Peach and green is a favorite color combo that I am pretty sure I inherited from Mama.

OPPOSITE: I love to use a sofa flanked by two chairs, anchored with a coffee table and two ottomans pulled up for extra seating. The existing pair of mirrors still remain and mimic the front windows.

ABOVE: A brandy board is a treasured piece in my stair hall, bridging the back hall and dining room. The pier mirror was the first antique I purchased when I graduated from Auburn. The pair of Pooky brass lamps add a nod to British style and complement the warm patinas.

RIGHT: I love how my dining room is now the central well of my home. An antique Oushak carpet grounds the space in fabulous tones of coral, citrine, lapis, and sage. I repurposed, reused, and rehung pieces I had, which makes the room familiar but fresh!

LEFT: I added mirrored transoms to the doors on both sides of the fireplace, allowing more light into the dining room. I perch at the island often, so this view through the dining room to the living room has become a most enjoyable scene. I moved the buffet and Louis Philippe mirror from Joe Pye Cottage to Farmdale. The lamps, by my friend Christopher Spitzmiller, are what I call "perfectly peach."

ABOVE: My stairwell niche is home to a mahogany bowfront chest—a classic choice for any room. The vintage vase became a lamp. The oil painting is by my friend David Baxter; cerulean, ruby, jade, and lush citrus hues are all concentrated in this still life.

PRECEDING: The same but different—that is a slogan in my design firm. My kitchen is the same—but different! It feels like home! Closed cabinetry to the ceiling elevates the volume, and the slab-front drawers provide wonderful storage. Melanie Herrington, in my office, designed the cabinets for me; ResCom Cabinetry constructed them; and my friend Dustin Weiche served as contractor (and probably therapist too) during the process.

ABOVE LEFT: My friends at Grace Rose Farm grow the most exquisite roses. This is "Beatrice," and it's stunning from bud to full bloom. The hand-painted bowl is from my aunt. My friend Eleanor Scott Davis painted the large abstract for me with all my favorite colors (also seen above right).

ABOVE RIGHT: My breakfast area is an homage to Mimi and Granddaddy's breakfast area. They always had a table with rolling chairs. Cabinet towers flank the front window and display my collection of creamware pieces.

OPPOSITE: A plaid by Colefax and Fowler dresses the chairs and window treatment. The morning light is fantastic in this niche.

OPPOSITE: My cooktop and sink are in the same position as before, which works for my cooking pattern and cleanup. The scallops in the cabinetry mimic the brick walkabout seen just outside the window. I used another favorite color combo of soft teal, tomato red, and creamy white for the plaid, rug, and cabinet colors.

ABOVE LEFT: Walnut countertops are warm and handsome on the perimeter. I designed the scalloped arched backsplash as a nod to the garden fountain wall.

ABOVE RIGHT: In my pantry, Cristi Flores painted a checkerboard-patterned floor reminiscent of older kitchens; I have a fondness for the pattern. The abstract, painted by my friend Allison James in shades of tangerine, sage, and powdery blue, adds a pop against the GP & J Baker wallpaper.

OPPOSITE: Two stacks of nostalgic views cap either end of the back hallway. At one end are countryside paintings reminiscent of my childhood farm, by local artist Butler Brown of Georgia. I added a large mirror on the long wall to reflect the garden and repeated the scalloped corner motif with it, thus reflecting the garden design.

LEFT: The other art stack, over my mother's secretary, is of Mediterranean harbor views in vibrant turquoise and terra-cotta, reminders of time there.

ABOVE: The "waller room" at Farmdale is where we love to relax. A favorite Sister Parish plaid on pillows adds a pop of blue. Brunschwig & Fils "Zambezi" used on club chairs is an all-time favorite animal print. Touches of green and orange are pulled from the Cowtan and Tout floral in the draperies and on pillows.

OPPOSITE: My sister Maggie painted the landscape in the center of the stack. The antique needlepoint chairs in the hallway are longtime favorite finds and inspired the waller room's palette. Sage green, terra-cotta, and soft blues are juxtaposed with the antique brick, raffia grass cloth, and painted rafters.

OPPOSITE: The stairwell wall is a gallery for my collection of floral paintings found here and there and everywhere over the years. My sweet friend Monteigne Mathison painted the zinnias and gifted them to me in memory of my grandmother, who also was a minister's wife and loved zinnias too.

ABOVE: A college friend and now acclaimed artist Emily York Ozier painted the large oil for me while I was building Farmdale. It now holds its place of honor in the loft of the stairwell. Lee Jofa "Tree of Life" upholsters a pair of chairs in this space, where I display nostalgic pieces of art and literature.

PRECEDING: My cabana and pool run parallel to Farmdale and connect the front and back gardens. I believe a landscape and garden should be laid out in rooms too. Its outdoor fireplace keeps the cabana in use during milder days.

LEFT: My friend and architect Brandon Ingram designed the pool cabana, which pays homage to one we both had seen and admired in childhood in Bainbridge, Georgia. The dining table between the cabana and pool is now the epicenter for summer birthdays, barbecues, and gatherings. Nitty Gritty roses in larger terra-cotta planters bloom from spring through fall. I designed the latticework planters flanking the cabana. All the seating is from Ballard Designs.

CAROLINA
ON
MY MIND

JOE PYE COTTAGE IS WONDERFUL
WHEN I'M HERE ALL ALONE AND EVEN
BETTER WHEN WE ARE ALL PILED IN AND
HAVING COFFEE ON THE PORCH.
IT'S A HAPPY HOME AWAY FROM HOME.

Many Southern families seek refuge from the heat and humidity of summertime in the mountains of North Carolina. My grandmother attended college in North Carolina and began visiting the mountains of western North Carolina then, later honeymooning there with my grandfather. My family still returns here to our homes for summertime and even stints in the fall for the grandeur of an Appalachian autumn. The tiny hamlet of Cashiers is where we have our homes—and like our homes in Perry, Georgia, that are on the same property, our homes in North Carolina are in the same neighborhood. It makes holidays and vacations so much fun!

My cottage in the mountains is affectionately dubbed Joe Pye Cottage—after my favorite native wildflower, the Joe Pye weed. And like the Joe Pye weed, which bolts and blossoms and changes with each season, my home in Cashiers has as well. I feel that interior designers go through phases and chapters with their own style and collections—some things remain the same for decades, and others change constantly. For me, I needed to rework some of the furniture for the way we live up here and how I entertain. I have found that bigger dinner parties always end up on the porch or deck to soak up the fabulous weather and be amidst the glorious surroundings. Breakfast and lunch are quick, efficient affairs—if we even sit down long enough to eat them. Chasing the kiddos, swimming, fishing, playing golf or pickleball, or taking long walks and fun hikes seems to fill our days. Our club is an easy walk or golf cart ride away, and so many of our meals depend on the day's activities.

We found that we needed room to enjoy conversation—a gathering spot by the fireplace to catch up and visit with our friends and family. I've had plans drawn for a larger kitchen and dining room addition, but that will be another season and chapter. Until then, I needed to embrace the footprint as is and tweak a few things. When we are all together, the television is not the center of attention. Conversation, games, and stoking the fire become the activities. I moved the TV into the former dining room, creating a cozy den. After all, it is usually only a couple of us watching when we do. The newly combined living and dining space makes the large living room multipurpose, and the small table becomes the perfect spot for a quick breakfast or simple lunch before hitting the courts or course. I also needed a larger bedroom for a downstairs guest room—and carving out the space by moving a door and window and wall provide the needed space. The square footage was there, so the guest room redo was doable.

One thing I love about Joe Pye Cottage is that it is wonderful when I'm here all alone and even better when we are all piled in and having coffee on the porch. It's a happy home away from home, and I think my grandparents would be thrilled to know their children and grandchildren love these mountains like they did. Carolina is often on my mind, and I cherish every season I can celebrate under those Carolina blue skies.

PAGES 190–191: A French cherry *bibliothèque*, or bookcase, now balances with the fireplace and displays some favorite pottery and ceramic pieces. I painted the interior of the bookcase a linen white—one of my favorite tricks of the trade for display pieces.

PRECEDING: Each year in September, I harvest hydrangeas for a large arrangement to display in my living room. They are a fond reminder of the wonderful season past. September is my favorite month in the mountains too. It is two parts summer, and one part fall. I collect white ironstone tureens and French *soupières*, and a few of my favorites are on display here.

OPPOSITE: I love having two smaller sofas near the fireplace for conversation and enjoying the fire. One of my personal favorite color combinations is a soft tan and coral with sage green, and I used that combination here with the sofas, pillows, and rug. Lee Jofa "Chinese Peony," the fabric that pulled all those colors together, is used on draperies and pillows.

ABOVE: The Lee Jofa "Chinese Peony" is hand-blocked on linen. A pair of watercolors I found at a local antique shop depict two of my favorite mountain flowers—daffodils and dahlias. The large picture window and doors in this room lead to the porch, so I used wicker chairs by Mainly Baskets as a nod to the porch furniture and nostalgic time spent there.

OPPOSITE: The scale of the oval French monastery table, moved from another spot, is great for this multipurpose room. Mimi's armchairs are my host and hostess chairs. The accent pillows are a Kravet terra-cotta linen. The large basket light fixture is a custom piece by Lowcountry Originals.

OPPOSITE: My dear friend Bee Sieburg painted the scene over the mantel, which captures the blooming flowers of June in the mountains. A favorite color combo of mine is mustard and mahogany, and my collection of English tea caddies and boxes go hand in hand with Vicki Miller pottery from Vivianne Metzger Antiques. A pair of antique wooden wine coolers host seasonal displays on the mantel.

ABOVE: A French cherry buffet is handsomely complemented with Carolina blue pottery lamps. A smattering of antique gamebird and waterfowl prints are matted in a mossy green and cream and framed in burnished gold. The sage-and-cream-striped wool rug is by Stark.

PAGES 200–203: I have a mantra of "green and white are always right" from gardening to tablescapes. Green chargers and Portuguese plates from Provvista help give me a base to build upon throughout the seasons. From spring tulips to summer dahlias, I love creating a tableau in the mountains.

PRECEDING: My former dining room is now a den and a great spot for the kiddos to watch a movie while the grown-ups chat by the fireplace in the adjacent living room. The Lee Jofa chintz includes a favorite combo of olive green, salmon, and teal.

ABOVE: An English mahogany bowfront chest is apropos and classic in any room. The Italian mirror has a cartouche that is

fondly reminiscent of my logo. A Mulberry Home plaid upholsters the wing chairs.

OPPOSITE: The first Bee Sieburg painting I ever purchased has a prominent place on the console table. The coral, citrine, and blue of the painting are echoed in the drapery and side chair.

OPPOSITE: A persimmon velvet by Brunschwig & Fils complements the velvet that is channel quilted on a sofa by Thibaut. The Lee Jofa "Trentham Hall" chintz is a crisp counterpoint to the velvet and wool plaid in the room. I found the side tables at Toby West Home.

ABOVE: A collection of old books and favorite reads fill up the shelves in the den. Fondly collected pieces of porcelain pottery and a small abstract by my friend Elaine Burge are on display. The fern frond candle sconces and framed fern prints are an homage to the wild ferns growing just outside the window.

ABOVE: I love that twelve antique bird prints I found and framed years ago have landed in my room at Joe Pye Cottage. The burled walnut frames and white matting with a handsome chocolate brown fillet set them apart from the background. The fabric and drapery is designed by noted interior designer and my friend Erika Powell.

RIGHT: A custom monogram on the shams was done by Joy Calwell at Initial Reaction, back home in Perry. The painting was a gift from one of my mother's best friends. The soothing blue on the ceiling is Benjamin Moore "Ice Cap." A favorite animal print by Jane Shelton upholsters the bench, and my friend Charlie West made the bedside lamps for me. I love the pistachio-hued speckles in the glaze!

OPPOSITE: Another favorite English chest of mine has aged with a perfect patina also seen in the mahogany-and-yew boxes. Mahogany and the mustard Vicki Miller lamps play well in my room.

ABOVE: My dear friend Libby Endry gifted me this Bee Sieburg painting. It depicts dahlias and zinnias in the glorious summertime of the mountains. A pair of French pine faux-bamboo chests serve as my nightstands and additional storage. "Squirrel and Sunflower" wallpaper by Mark Hearld, in green sedge, was one of the first things I selected for this home years ago, and I still adore it today!

ABOVE: A painted English bowfront chest was found at Madison Markets in Madison, Georgia. A handsome inlaid teak and mother-of-pearl octagonal mirror anchors a wall in the guest room, while a vintage brass deer is now an admired lamp. I used Benjamin Moore "Creekside Green" for the trim and baseboards.

RIGHT: The new guest suite is awash in sage and tan and cream. A painted stripe by Thibaut dresses the walls, and I reworked the Thibaut linen with ferns on the window. Kravet nightstands flank the faux-bamboo bed I had made. A Bee Sieburg painting presides over the bed and was the launch for the palette in the room. Ice buckets from the old High Hampton Inn are perfect vessels for ferns and bedside greenery.

ABOVE: My sweet friend Eliza Price painted the fern fronds for me when she was in college. The house was furnished when I purchased it, and I kept this wonderful faux-bamboo painted chair, which holds a stack of reads for guests to enjoy.

OPPOSITE: A framed landscape by Lauren Smith is displayed atop an English pine drop-leaf table that was one of the first antiques I bought. A favorite pair of pottery vases sport a Chelsea Textiles check for their shades.

AMERICANA
WITH
A TWIST

CHANNELING THE NAUTICAL HISTORY
OF THE ISLAND—THE TIGHT QUARTERS
OF SAILORS, LOBSTERMEN, AND
FISHERMEN—INSPIRED A COZY CABIN VIBE
FOR THIS ADORABLE COTTAGE.

Quintessential Americana design, decor, and delights can be found on Martha's Vineyard, from the cedar shakes and white picket fences to the bunting and flags. It seems like even the gardens and landscaping echo something patriotic, coloring the landscape with red geraniums, white daisies, and blue hydrangeas. For a young family's new home away from home on Martha's Vineyard, I channeled this trio of colors but with a twist! Coral, cream, and cerulean—inspired by red, white, and blue—create a lively yet soothing palette for the cottage.

Tucked in the hamlet of Edgartown, the property drew our clients in not only for its proximity to town but its family orientation, with a grandparent just across the street! Walkable excursions to dinner, shopping, and gatherings with relatives sealed the deal for this family, and the promise of a project was soon underway! Having known this family for many years and loving them as dear friends, I relished creating a home for them while spending time on this ever-so-charming island. From Perry to the ferry—I love the planes, trains, and automobiles of the journey there. I knew that traveling to a place to call home on this island was paramount for my clients and friends.

Channeling the nautical history of the island—the tight quarters of sailors, lobstermen, and fishermen—inspired a cozy cabin vibe for this adorable cottage. Painted floors in tones of cream and blue and woven wall coverings in decking stripes all pay homage to the bars and stripes, while accents of coral, persimmon, and garnet lend a nod to red.

For the main room, I was inspired by the gambrel and barn rooflines seen around the island. Painted rafters and boards add lofty volume, while the woven plaid rug atop old-fashioned, checkerboard-painted floors grounds the seating area. A series of shelving display nautical treasures, books, and objets d'art pertinent to the personality of Martha's Vineyard as well as the family. An aqua-and-white leafy-pattern wallcovering sets the vibrant tone of the room and is juxtaposed with toffee-hued plaid on the windows. The bedrooms are "jam up and jelly tight," with nautical-inspired stripes setting the tone in each room.

This home serves as a guesthouse when the grandparent's home is full. What I love so much about this home is that it lives large—smaller in its footprint but greatly impacting those who lodge there, whether for a couple of nights or a season.

So, here is a place for a family to be together during intentionally slower summer days—walking to lunch or dinner, seeing grandparents and friends who are just across the street, no hurry to get here and there but a pace more leisurely and luxurious than is currently at hand. This is the intention for finding home again—to truly find the delight in each season of life. Plus, a picnic lunch of lobster rolls helps anyplace feel like home.

PAGE 218: For the family room, a multipurpose space is awash in pops of persimmon, creamy linen, and shades of sky blue. Flanking the stairwell, a pair of commissioned paintings by Erin Clark.

PRECEDING: For the entryway, a kitchenette and bar serves its function for long weekends and Fourth of July overflow from the family's main house. The still life is by artist Kate Comen Freeman. My team designed the cabinetry and had the walls and ceiling painted to match.

ABOVE: A vestibule off the main living area is a playful mix of checks and stripes.

OPPOSITE: A living room corner is set for games or breakfast. The home's color scheme is reiterated by artist Erin Clark. Indochine-style armchairs are pulled up to the mid-century tulip table. Sailor's knots and concentric squares add detail to the draperies, all constructed by Julie Thome. The custom area rug is by Elizabeth Eakins.

ABOVE: A George Spencer Designs toffee check contrasts with the leaf-motif wallpaper. A pair of French oil paintings were reframed for the project by Ocmulgee Arts. The sofa, in an exaggerated caning pattern, can be turned into a bed for extra company. Pillows, lampshades, and swivel chairs wear a soft blue stripe.

OPPOSITE: Custom built-ins and registers designed by my team anchor one whole end of the living room. Shelves are home to collected mementos from travels, favorite reads, gifts from the sea, and other objets d'art. The painted rafters and boards are reminiscent of a ship's hull and ribbing.

OPPOSITE: The backs of the built-ins are painted a soft green as a wonderful backdrop to the books, shells, and pottery. The register has a fan pattern that takes on the shape of waves.

LEFT: A North Star was painted in the vestibule between the living room and adjoining bedroom. All the painted floors in the home have a pattern or detail nostalgic of New England–style painted floors.

BELOW: The vintage rattan-and-bamboo coffee table, with a fresh coat of lacquer, is a curated plane of the location and season. The vintage, bobbin-leg stool tucked under the table has a new bit of ikat-patterned upholstery.

OVERLEAF: A custom made-to-measure and painted console table sports a pair of tortoiseshell rattan lamps. Hydrangeas of Martha's Vineyard are outstanding in the summer and have turned glorious shades of red, chartreuse, and coral after the season. A pair of Queen Anne–style side chairs in coordinating ticking stripe add a warm patina to the room. A framed TV hangs on the shelves.

A HOME to SHARE

STYLE COMFORT HOME   ANDREW HOWARD

OPPOSITE: The guest suite is designed to be jam up and jelly tight! We used a stripe to paper the walls and ceiling and for the drapery fabric too. We painted the trim in a smoky blue. An antique portrait of a sea captain is a nod to the history of the island. A large piece by artist Blakely Made is titled *Sea Treasures*.

ABOVE: In the guest bath, a custom vanity is topped with muddy veined marble, which was also used to fabricate the sink. We designed the shell motif logo for the house and applied it to linens. The porthole mirror is a nod to ship windows, and the frond-motif paper is by Anna French.

OPPOSITE: Built-ins frame the upholstered bed and provide storage in this "cabin," inspired by rooms on a boat. A whale by artist Mary McGuire hangs over the headboard. Lampshade fabric, Euro pillows, and shams add softness and more pattern to the room.

ABOVE: A grid of Mary McGuire's pieces adds pops of color to the room. For the lead edge of the draperies, we used a blue-and-white tape with a brush fringe. The ceiling is papered in the same stripe as the walls but cut into concentric squares—a favorite trick of the trade for use with stripes.

ABOVE: In the "captain's quarters," a soothing palette of aloe blue and tan creates a serene backdrop. The whitewashed bed's headboard is upholstered in a robin's-egg blue check. The sets of double doors hide a stacked washer and dryer and closet space; the panels are shirred with the same check used on the bed and lampshades.

OPPOSITE: This primary suite had some exquisite details, from the flower registers to the hand-painted floors. Complementing tones of cream-and-tan stripes in the wallpaper are offset with aloe-blue trim. Tortoiseshell bamboo side tables are handsome complements to drapery in a fern and frond motif. The diamond pattern wool rug is a smaller scale and similar pattern to the checkerboard-painted floor. A smattering of oyster shell plates and scalloped plates hang over antique engravings of ships in the harbor.

OPPOSITE: An aqua trellis by Schumacher creates pattern in this en suite primary bath. The slab-panel drawers and cabinets are accented in a reed detail. Ivory-colored, ceramic faux-bamboo pieces create a striking frame on the vanity mirrors. Antique paintings of ships have new frames, for a fresh take on a classic genre.

LEFT: More oyster plates and scalloped plates add a pop of crispness, and the window shade coordinates with the draperies in the primary bedroom.

BELOW: A deep-coral ceramic tile was laid in an ashlar pattern on the floor and in a honeycomb for the shower floor. The ceiling is painted a faded bluish green. An antique mahogany stool with a rush top serves as a towel holder. I love the warmth of this patina against the crisp blues.

ACKNOWLEDGMENTS

I am proof of the adage "It takes a village to raise a child"—and producing a book is no exception! My "village" is a lovely group of friends and family, collaborators and teammates, tradesmen and artists, editors and publisher, and, of course, talented people all around who I have the pleasure of working with on each project.

My family inspires and encourages me and gives me the creative outlet to feather a nest for us all. Maggie and Zach and their children, Leyla, Napp, Sarah, Keyla, and Sally James, fill my home with love and laughter each holiday and during wonderful weekends together. Meredith and Keaton and their children, Jack and Margaret, also fill Farmdale and Joe Pye Cottage with much joy! I love being "Brubbs" to my nieces and nephews and to my delightful and growing tribe of cousins and their families as well!

Thank you to my aunt and uncle, Kathy and Gerry Brantley, aka Bee and Papa, who provide such a loving example of acceptance, like Mimi and Granddaddy did.

Frank Martin, you provide steadiness and love for me—devotion that I could not imagine would be possible. Thank you for loving me for who I am—as I'm thrilled to love you as the brilliant and wonderful man you are. And thank you for always encouraging me to learn and grow.

My team at James Farmer Inc. allows me the absolute privilege of creating and dreaming and facilitating those ideas into lovely homes for our dear clients and customers. Jesse Noble, Haley Yarbrough, Melanie Herrington, Ashley Hulbert, Margaret Keyes, Melissa Sparrow, Ellen Palmer, Laura Medlin, Mary Margaret Tuggle, Lizzie Grace, Angela Westmoreland, Kathy James, and Gracie Potts—ladies, y'all are beyond amazing, and I cannot thank you enough for the honor of working with you!

To my incredibly talented friend and photographer Emily Followill, thank you for capturing our work and being the dearest friend too! You and Kelly Blackmon make an awesome team, and our travels and photo shoots are all the more fun because y'all make them truly delightful!

To the workrooms, contractors, fabric houses, installers, and craftsmen who fabricate so much—thank you! And to our fabulous seamstresses—thank you! Julie Thome works wonders

for us! Mrs. Ruth Moss has nearly raised me since I was a kid! And, of course, Rosie Jacobs, whose cheeriness always brightens our day! Thank you to Lanier Mitchell, who hangs anything that will sit still—along with draperies and art. You're a friend and magician!

Thank you, Susie Williams, for keeping me and Farmdale going! And thank you, Brenda Simon for helping me make the garden grow and glow!

Our clients become friends and dearest people to my team and me. Thank you for allowing us the utmost honor of serving you and creating places to call home for you and your families. Turns out, you can go home again! Mary and Dave Cyr, Candice and the late Marty Carr, Julie and David Blount, Heather and Philip McWane, Anne and Tim Norwood, Elyse and Andrew Starling, Elizabeth and Kevin Phillips—thank you for trusting us. We are truly grateful for you and your families. Thank you to my longtime friend and client Mrs. Betty Lanier, who truly gave me a start!

Thank you to Gibbs Smith for believing in me from the start and for continued support. Madge Baird, you are my North Star! Thank you for bringing dreams and visions to print and, thus, to life. Congrats on your outstanding career and anniversary of fifty years with Gibbs Smith. I am thrilled for our next projects!

First Edition
29 28 27 26 25   5 4 3 2 1

Published by
Gibbs Smith
570 N. Sportsplex Drive
Kaysville, Utah 84037
1.800.835.4993 orders
www.gibbs-smith.com

Designed by Rita Sowins/Sowins Design

Library of Congress Control Number: 2024952097
ISBN: 978-1-4236-6746-9

Printed and bound in China
This product is made of FSC®-certified and other controlled material.